Research on the EDGE

RAINFORESTS

LOUISE SPILSBURY

WAYLAND

First published in 2014 by Wayland

Copyright © Wayland 2014

Wayland
338 Euston Road
London NW1 3BH

Wayland Australia
Level 17/207 Kent Street
Sydney, NSW 2000

Produced for Wayland by Calcium
Edited by Sarah Eason and Jennifer Sanderson
Design concept and cover design by Lisa Peacock
Page layout by Keith Williams

Picture acknowledgements
Cover: Corbis: Pete Oxford/Minden Pictures main; Shutterstock: Christopher Meder top; Inside: Dreamstime: Adifor 11b, Nateskate66 18b, Paura 11t, Spphotos 18t, 24b; Forest Stewardship Council: 26t; Getty Images: Tengku Bahar/ AFP 9, Timothy G. Laman/National Geographic 8; Istockphoto: Guenterguni 17; Shutterstock: 7, Silvano Audisio 23b, Stephane Bidouze 1, 23t, Dirk Ercken 20b, Frontpage 29, Gopause 22, Ben Heys 19, Kjersti Joergensen 28b, Dmitry Kalinovsky 25, NH 5t, Boivin Nicolas 28t, Orange Line Media 21, Vadim Petrakov 20t, Scott Prokop 26b, Alexander Raths 27, Dr. Morley Read 10, 13t, Lisette van der Hoorn 6, Kirsanov Valeriy Vladimirovich 16b, Worldswildlifewonders 13b, Adam Ziaja 24t, Egon Zitter 5t; Wikimedia Commons: Nireekshit 12, Vaikoovery 14–15.

Dewey number: 333.7'5-dc23
ISBN: 978 0 7502 8013 6

Printed in China

10 9 8 7 6 5 4 3 2 1

Wayland is a division of Hachette Children's Books,
an Hachette UK company.
www.hachette.co.uk

CONTENTS

WORKING IN A RAINFOREST

Hot, steamy, rainy, overgrown, muddy, thorny, full of biting insects and other animals that can cause harm... Rainforests are extreme environments, yet some scientists work there every day, researching plants, animals, soils and other aspects of these wild, remote places.

A Study in Biodiversity

Rainforests are natural laboratories with incredible biodiversity, from enormous trees to tiny orchids and millions of different animals living in, on or among the plants. Scientists study in rainforests to learn more about the remarkable organisms that live there and how they interact. They also hope to discover new species, partly because these discoveries may help scientists to develop new medicines and materials.

Scientists research tropical rainforests to try to improve our understanding of the unique plants and animals in this amazing ecosystem.

DANGER!

Tens of millions of species of insect live in rainforests. Some are just irritating but others can harm researchers. For example, tiny sweat bees crowd onto any uncovered flesh to lick salt from sweat, while bot flies lay their eggs under human skin. Stings from wild rainforest bees and bullet ants are extremely painful.

What Scientists Study

Scientists also find out how the changes to forests that are caused by people, such as deforestation, affect the climate and the forest water supply. Working with foreign governments and local people, scientists use their findings to conserve rainforests worldwide. In this book, we will look at how the scientists carry out their research, what they do with their results and some of the discoveries they have made.

Colourful pitcher plants grow on the mossy branches of rainforest trees.

> Rhinoceros beetles look fearsome but they are harmless to people. The male's large horns are used to fight other males in the rainforest.

RAINFOREST LIFE

Thousands of different scientists work in rainforests every year, each with a different research focus. They come to the rainforest because of the immense biodiversity and because rainforests, and the organisms within them, are disappearing.

▼ Rainforest trees are mostly hardwoods that are valuable but can be slow-growing. Once logged, the rainforest does not re-grow quickly and some tree species die out.

Rainforests Under Pressure

Some researchers study threats to rainforest wildlife. For example, while rainforest animals are under threat from hunters who kill them for meat, hunting affects plants in the forest, too. In 2010, researchers proved that the poaching of elephants was linked to a loss of trees such as the star apple. This is because after eating the fruit, the elephants spread the seeds of these trees through their droppings.

Jaguars are hunted for their beautiful coats but are also disappearing as people kill the animals jaguars hunt for food.

Rainforest Discovery

Scientists also study tropical rainforests to find new species. Rainforests are home to half of the world's estimated 10 million plant and animal species. So far, scientists think they have discovered only about 6 per cent of these, and they are finding new things all the time. In 2008, researchers using Google Earth even spotted a completely new area of rainforest on Mount Mabu in Mozambique that had never before been charted!

DANGER!

Scientists in the field have to look out for forest elephants, particularly in some African rainforests, where elephant attacks are increasing. Elephants are not naturally aggressive but because forests are shrinking, they are more likely to meet and be scared by people, such as farmers protecting their fields.

RAINFOREST GEAR

Scientists working in the rainforest use a variety of equipment, depending on their field of research.

Traps to Thermometers

Scientists studying wildlife need to collect or view animals to study. To do this, they may use pooters, which are tubes that suck up and collect insects and other small animals. Light traps are lit-up sheets that attract insects, such as moths, at night. Camera traps automatically take a photograph of any animal that breaks an infrared light beam. Scientists studying the weather use thermometers, rainfall gauges and humidity and gas sensors. They determine locations using GPS devices. Most scientists record data and observations using notebooks and pens, laptops, cameras and sound recorders.

▼ Moths are attracted to light so researchers set up simple light traps like this one. A light is suspended in front of a white sheet and the moths fly onto the sheet where they can be examined.

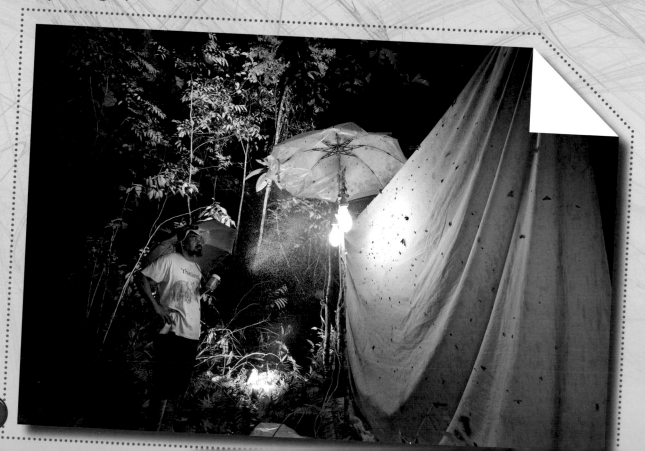

Facing Challenges

The rainforest climate can damage some equipment or make it tricky to use. For example, water vapour from the high humidity can easily fog camera lenses. Water, dust or small ants get into laptops, cameras and mobile phones, causing the machines to overheat, or electronic damage that stops the devices from working. Even the labs are under threat as wooden buildings can be eaten away by invading termites!

This tapir has been fitted with a radio transmitter collar that scientists can use to track its movements in the Malaysian rainforest where it lives.

CUTTING EDGE

Keeping sight of animals is tricky in dense rainforests so scientists use wireless telemetry. They attach or surgically implant light radio transmitters in animals and then use hand-held aerials and radios to track the direction and strength of the signal from the transmitters. Computers are used to record and analyze movement data and display results.

ROUGH AND REMOTE

The quickest, easiest way for researchers to reach their isolated rainforest research labs is usually by boat. In rainforest regions with few rivers or no major roads, scientists often take a helicopter from the nearest city to their research site.

Walk to Work

When they have been dropped off, scientists may be able to travel the rest of the journey by road or they may have to walk to their research station. Walking causes the least damage or disruption to remote habitats. However, walking through the rainforest is slow progress, partly because fast-growing vines and branches clog up trails. Researchers often have to hack their way through tough forest undergrowth with sharp machetes.

Rainforest, such as this area surrounding the Amazon river, is so thick that trails can easily become overgrown.

CUTTING EDGE

Remote labs have poor or non-existent mobile phone and landline coverage so scientists keep in touch with others using satellite phones. These transmit and receive voice and data signals to and from satellites orbiting Earth. The phones are small and cheap so even scientists working with low research budgets can use them.

Scientists use kayaks and inflatable boats to travel and bring equipment and supplies to remote rainforest settlements where ferry services are infrequent.

Four-by-fours must carry fuel supplies and tools to mend vehicles – there are few garages and recovery vehicles in the rainforest!

Road Problems

Many of the roads researchers have to travel on in rainforests are rough, winding mud tracks with no tarmac. Some are pitted with deep, wide holes, which damage vehicles that drive into them. Rainstorms often wash away stretches of road completely. Scientists usually use four-by-fours and other vehicles with knobbly tyres to grip rough roads. Some vehicles even have aerial exhaust pipes so they do not suck up muddy water when travelling through puddles.

RESPECTING THE FOREST

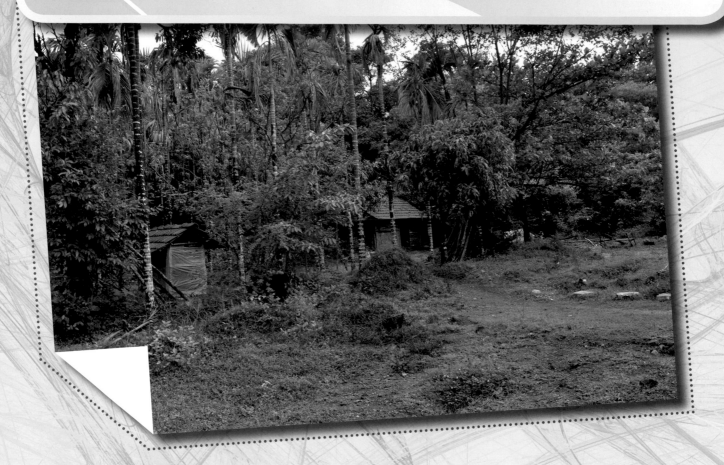

When scientists live and work in the rainforest they have to take care not to damage the very things – plants, wildlife and environment – they have come to research.

Reducing Impacts

To avoid cutting down trees for fuel, scientists cook on kerosene stoves or solar cookers, which use shiny surfaces to intensify heat from sunlight onto a cooking vessel. They carefully remove

▲ Lab buildings can be made from local timber. Fences to keep out wild animals are made of smooth wire that will not injure wildlife.

rubbish, such as plastic bags or tins, which can trap and harm rainforest animals. For building, they try to use local materials that are renewable or in high supply rather than bringing in lorry-loads of materials made elsewhere, which would cause pollution and the need to build more roads.

Protecting the Canopy

More than two-thirds of all organisms in the rainforest live in the canopy, the highest parts of the trees that can be 30 metres (98.4 feet) above the ground. In the past, scientists studied canopy life by felling trees or spraying chemicals to kill or stun animals so they dropped to the ground. Today, they use less invasive techniques. Mountaineering equipment allows scientists to reach high branches safely. Researchers also construct canopy walkways, observation towers and platforms.

Fixed bridges let scientists move between rainforest trees without any risk of damaging branches and the plants and animals that live and grow on them.

CUTTING EDGE

In 2012, architect Yi Yvonne Weng designed a Canopy Trail. This is a light mesh of carbon fibre and metal rods rather like a spider's web that can be spread over the canopy. Scientists can use tear-drop-shaped pods suspended from the mesh as mobile labs between the trees.

13

RAINFOREST LAB

Scientists working in rainforests need buildings in which to live, plan and discuss their research, and store and study the samples and collected data. They do this in research stations or labs.

Different Shapes and Sizes

There is a huge range of rainforest labs. Some are just tents or tarpaulins stretched over branches. Others are large buildings with well-equipped labs, classrooms, canteens and bedrooms. Most labs are in remote places, so staff set up systems to clean water for drinking, dispose of waste and generate electricity by photovoltaic (PV) panels, which use the abundant sunlight of a rainforest.

Agumbe, India

Agumbe Rainforest Research Station (ARRS) in south-west India is a typical rainforest lab. Its facilities include a laboratory where researchers study local wildlife such as king cobras, and a small library and reading room. There is also an office for the director of ARRS.

The living areas of Agumbe include dormitories with bunk beds for visiting scientists and conservation volunteers, a lounge with chairs and tables, and a basic kitchen with a cooker, sink and preparation area. There is no fridge because the power supply is variable.

Surrounding the main building are a toilet and shower block with solar-heated water, cottages for resident staff and a garden in which food is grown. The Station has a four-by-four and motorbikes to pick up visitors, fetch supplies and for emergencies – the nearest hospital is more than 30 kilometres (18.6 miles) away.

Agumbe Rainforest Research Station is a simple building with a watertight roof to keep out heavy rainforest rainfall.

CUTTING EDGE

Daintree Research Station in Australia has a 47-metre (154-foot) crane with a long arm and platform at the top. The crane can rotate 360 degrees so that scientists can study an area of the upper rainforest measuring 1 hectare (11,960 square yards).

Scientists observe and track forest wildlife from the crane platform at Daintree Research Station.

LIFE IN THE LAB

Scientists working in the rainforest need to dress appropriately for the conditions. Many wear long-sleeved shirts and trousers to protect their skin from sunburn and scratches or rashes caused by thorny, poisonous plants and biting insects. Sunscreen and insect repellents are also essential. Scientists wear comfortable boots to prevent blisters because in humid, dirty rainforest conditions, a small blister can become a painful wound if it is infected.

After a day of observation and data collection, scientists gather to eat a meal before further scientific study in the evening.

Using a head torch or light trap at night allows scientists to attract and study nocturnal animals, but they may also attract stinging or irritating insects.

On the Lookout

In the rainforest people need to constantly be aware of dangers. For example, they check their boots before putting them on in case a scorpion or venomous centipede has crawled inside. They also always check with locals before venturing into a rainforest river — there is always the danger that stingrays, piranhas or caimans are in the water!

Scientists may patiently observe worms in the wild for long periods until they gather enough data to reveal patterns of behaviour.

Scientific Research

It can be fascinating and thrilling to study rainforests but it is also usually time-consuming. Rainforest scientists rarely have a day off. Locating organisms to study within a rainforest can take many days, and evenings may be spent writing notes, studying in the library and examining samples collected during the day.

DANGER!

Fungi grow on any warm, damp surface, from clothing and food to people's feet. Foot rot is a fungal infection that gets a grip when feet are never properly dry. In the rainforest, scientists have to wash their feet and socks daily. They also dry their feet carefully and apply ointment or powder to keep foot rot at bay.

PEOPLE OF THE RAINFOREST

There are around 50 million tribal people living in the world's rainforests, most of them in the vast Amazon rainforest of South America. Researchers can learn much from working with these people as many survive in part on forest resources such as wood and wild honey.

> Long ago, South American tribes discovered that some rainforest trees produce milky latex when their bark is cut. Today people use latex to make products such as rubber and chewing gum.

This rainforest guide is using a leaf to drink fresh water naturally stored within a tree trunk.

Knowledge Base

Rainforest tribes, especially their healers and shamans, have expert knowledge of forest plants and animals that is passed down through generations. A single Amazonian tribe, such as the Yanomani, may use more than 200 different plants as medicines. Many of the medicines we use today, such as aspirin, were discovered when scientists studied how rainforest tribes use plants.

Local Skills

Researchers also rely on local people in other ways. For example, they may buy food, mosquito nets and insect repellent from local businesses. They employ local people as cooks or expert animal trackers. Scientists setting up canopy walkways or research centres may also help to establish tourism businesses run by local people, who act as guides and give talks to visitors about their land and cultures. Scientists often rely on tribal people to help them locate new species, and to learn more about known ones.

Tribal people use their detailed knowledge of the routes and organisms of the rainforest to lead groups of visitors around.

DANGER!

Locals know which rainforest plants to avoid. For example, the stinging tree has fine, poisonous hairs on its leaves that can give people painful rashes for two months. The finger cherry can cause blindness if eaten and raw cashew nuts are highly poisonous.

RICHES OF THE RAINFOREST

Each year, research scientists find about 2,000 new rainforest species and discover more about existing rainforest organisms, too.

New Species

Most discoveries are of small animals, such as new beetles and spiders, but large animals are found, too. New species of giant rat, monkey, parrot, dolphin and anaconda were just a few of the 1,200 species discovered in the Amazon rainforest between 1999 and 2009.

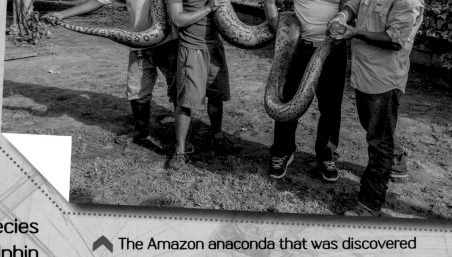

The Amazon anaconda that was discovered in 2009 was the first anaconda species found worldwide since 1936. It can grow to 4 metres (13 feet) long and it hunts caimans and jaguars.

Some drugs, such as the muscle relaxant tubocurarine, are derived from the poisonous skin of certain rainforest treefrogs.

DANGER!

Scientists discovered that some rainforest frogs release poisons through their skin to stop animals eating them. These are also lethal to humans. An amount of poison the size of a grain of salt from the golden poison arrow frog can cause death.

Finding New Medicines

Some rainforest scientists research the chemicals in plants, especially the toxins or poisons, which might be useful in medicines. For example, a plant with bark which fungi do not grow on, and that insects do not eat, because of the toxins it contains, is used in medicine to treat rheumatism. About 1 per cent of all plants have been screened for useful chemicals for medicines, yet one-quarter of all drugs are derived from rainforest ingredients, including two anti-cancer drugs from the poisonous rosy periwinkle plant of Madagascar (see page 24).

Many medicines are made from or inspired by substances found in rainforest plant, animal and insect species. When these medicines are taken by or injected into patients, they can save lives.

GLOBAL AIR CONDITIONER

Researchers have discovered that rainforests help to control gases, temperature and water levels in the atmosphere around Earth. They are rather like a global air conditioning system!

Gas Exchange

Trees take in carbon dioxide and water, and release oxygen in the process of photosynthesis. Using gas sensors on individual leaves, scientists have estimated that the Amazon rainforest alone stores 90 to 140 billion tonnes (100 to 157 tons) of carbon, mostly as wood, and releases 20 per cent of the world's oxygen. Deforestation reduces the oxygen supply because there are fewer trees, and it also creates more carbon dioxide, for example when trees are burned to clear land. The extra carbon dioxide in the atmosphere, added to that which is released by burning fossil fuels to power machines, is thought to cause global warming.

The water rainforests produce and hold is vital for rainforest wildlife.

Rainforests and Water

Researchers have discovered that a rainforest creates up to 75 per cent of its own rainfall in a closed system. Water in canopy leaves evaporates fast in high rainforest temperatures and this water vapour condenses on bacteria in the atmosphere above, forming clouds. Rain falls from the clouds back down into forest soil, rivers and streams. However, this system is being broken down by deforestation. Fewer trees means less rainfall, so streams dry up, plants die and soil (no longer bound by plant roots) is blown or washed away by storms.

Lush rainforest vegetation benefits from the constant supply of water in the rainforest's unique water system.

Rainforests are named for the rain clouds they create above them.

CUTTING EDGE

In some rainforests researchers use networks of sensors on cables strung between towers to automatically monitor temperature, humidity, rainfall and carbon dioxide levels. Data from the sensors reveals the interaction between the forest and atmosphere in more detail than from a single monitoring point.

BILLIuN-DOLLAR FuREsT

Drugs companies can make huge profits from selling medicines they produce from rainforest species.

It costs a great deal of money to build and run rainforest labs and to pay for research equipment and scientists' salaries. Hundreds of governments, companies and charities spend billions of dollars each year on rainforest research.

bio-prospecting. They do this partly because they can sell the medicines for a lot of money. For example, the drug company Eli Lilly earned around US$100 million each year for decades from sales of its anti-cancer drugs derived from the rainforest rosy periwinkle. Using these anti-cancer drugs has increased the survival of children with leukemia from 20 to 80 per cent.

Bio-Prospecting

Drug companies and medical charities fund research into new active ingredients for medicines. This is called

Local people, such as this boy from Equatorial Guinea, can benefit from the money large companies pay to research the rainforest.

Owning Forest

Some drug companies pay bio-prospecting fees to governments or organizations in the countries in which they research. For example, in 1992, drug company Merck paid a Costa Rican research centre more than US$1 million to supply plants and insects for its drug-screening programmes. Merck also agreed to pay a percentage of profits on any drug sales resulting from Costa Rican organisms. When a company has designed a new medicine, it applies for a patent. This gives the company exclusive use of its invention. This exclusivity can earn the company millions of dollars.

Drugs discovered in rainforests are developed in labs in other countries and then manufactured in different places.

CUTTING EDGE

In 2009, researchers at the Carnegie Institution for Science developed a system of sensors to create 3-D maps of the chemicals in rainforest plants from small aeroplanes. Spotting the promise of the system, the Gordon and Betty Moore Foundation awarded the researchers more than US$5 million to improve the technology so it is possible to identify plants by their chemical 'fingerprint'.

SHARING SCIENCE

After scientists have collected and studied data and compiled the results of their research, they share those findings with fellow scientists, governments and other organizations to make a difference to people's lives.

Acting on Results

After scientists have collected and studied data, they write up their findings in journals or present them at conferences to share and compare them with discoveries made by other scientists. Then they pass on findings to newspapers and other media,

When people buy wood products, such as paper, marked with this FSC logo they know that buying them will not mean harming the world's forests.

governments and charities so that the facts can be used to bring about change. For example, after researchers revealed the dangers of deforestation in the 1980s, the Forest Stewardship Council (FSC)® was set up in 1993. This international, non-profit organization checks that trees are being felled legally and in a way that does not damage the forests, the people who live in them and the wider environment.

Your Work

These Earth scientists are sharing the valuable information that each one has discovered in his or her specialist area.

A scientist may work alone in his or her lab but sharing research is vital.

Plant to Medicine

When scientists discover plants that could be used for medicines, they either pass on their discoveries or work with other scientists testing those chemicals in laboratories. They have to test doses required, how well they work and if they cause side effects. They may do this by testing the drugs on micro-organisms, animals or human volunteers. This process can take 10 to 15 years before the medicines are licensed for sale. It is a long process involving many scientists and there are many failures: on average, only 250 out of 20,000 plants tested prove useful.

CUTTING EDGE

Researchers are testing lesser-known species of tree to see how hard-wearing they are. These can be sold to building companies and manufacturers instead of them using the precious rainforest trees that are becoming more rare.

SECRETS OF THE RAINFOREST

Researchers have already discovered some of the secrets of the rainforests and if they get the chance, they are likely to discover many more. Some of these discoveries, such as new medicines, directly benefit humankind and others enrich people's lives.

⌃ What amazing medicines, foods and other products might researchers yet discover can be made from the rainforest riches?

⌃ Orangutans spend about 90 per cent of their lives in trees but because of hunting and logging, these apes are now in danger of extinction.

Saving Our Future

Scientists have shown that forests currently absorb around 10 per cent of the world's carbon dioxide emissions. Perhaps the most important research scientists are doing into rainforests today is what will happen if too many trees are cut and burned down. Many believe that if forests die and are replaced by bushes and shrubs that do not create their own rainfall system, these plants will dry out in the heat and be prone to fire. If this happens, rainforest regions will stop halting global warming and could even accelerate it.

Saving People, Saving Rainforests

There are still many species of plant yet to be discovered and researched in the rainforest, some of which could be vital in fighting disease. This means that rainforest land has much more economic value today, and more potential than timber and farmland to make money in the future. With this information, governments might sign up to protecting rainforests in the future.

▼ Researchers are trying to find ways to balance the demands of business, such as farming, with the needs of the rainforest.

CUTTING EDGE

Some researchers are studying how fungi that grows on rubber trees in the Amazon rainforest produces chemicals that break down plastics. They believe this could be part of the solution to the worldwide problem of disposing of plastic waste.

GLOSSARY

atmosphere The layer of gases surrounding Earth.

bacteria A single-celled, microscopic, plant-like organism.

biodiversity The variety of plant and animal life in a particular habitat or ecosystem.

cancer A disease caused by an uncontrolled spread of abnormal cells in the body.

canopy The top layer of trees and branches in a forest.

carbon dioxide A gas in the atmosphere that is linked to global warming.

climate The usual pattern of weather that happens in a place.

condenses Changes from a gas into liquid (such as water vapour to water).

conservation The protection of something endangered such as rainforest.

data Information such as facts and statistics.

deforestation Cutting or burning down large areas of trees.

ecosystem A community of plants and animals and their physical surroundings.

emissions Gases released into the atmosphere.

evaporates Changes from a liquid into a gas (such as water to water vapour).

fungi A living thing that grows on other plants or rotting matter.

global warming Changes in the Earth's weather patterns caused by human activity.

GPS (Global Positioning System) A system that uses signals from satellites in Space to locate positions on Earth.

humidity The amount of water vapour in the air.

infrared A type of light that is invisible.

media Newspapers, television, Internet and other ways in which information is relayed to the public.

micro-organisms Microscopic living things.

organism A living thing.

oxygen A gas in the atmosphere that living things need to breathe.

patent A licence that gives a company or individual the exclusive rights to an invention for a set period of time.

photosynthesis The process by which plants make food from carbon dioxide and water using energy from sunlight.

photovoltaic The process that produces electricity from sunlight.

pollution When air, soil or water are spoiled or made dirty or harmful by something else.

renewable Something that can be replaced.

rheumatism A painful disorder of the joints or muscles.

satellites Man-made pieces of equipment that orbit Earth.

sensors Devices that detect and measure something such as amounts of a particular gas in the air.

species A particular type of plant or animal.

toxins Poisons made by animals or plants.

water vapour When water is a gas in the air. Water comes in three states: water vapour (gas), water (liquid water) and ice (solid water).

FURTHER READING

Books

Amazing Animal Adaptions: Rainforest Animal Adaptations. Lisa Amstutz, Capstone Press, 2012.

Discover More: Rainforest. Penny Arlon, Scholastic, 2013.

Explorer Travel Guides: Rainforests. Nick Hunter, Raintree, 2013.

Mapping Global Issues: Rainforest Destruction. Peter Littlewood, Franklin Watts, 2012.

Unstable Earth: What Happens If the Rainforests Disappear? Mary Colson, Wayland, 2013.

Websites

Read about a day in the life of a rainforest scientist at:
www.nasa.gov/centers/ames/research/factsheets/FS-021101ARC.html

Find out where rainforests of the world are at:
www.srl.caltech.edu/personnel/krubal/rainforest/Edit560s6/www/where.html

Read news and facts and watch videos about rainforests at:
www.bbc.co.uk/nature/habitats/Tropical__and__subtropical__moist__broadleaf__forests

Watch a short video about how and why the FSC was set up at:
www.fsc-uk.org/our-history.26.htm

INDEX

Research on the EDGE

978 0 7502 8014 3

978 0 7502 8016 7

978 0 7502 8013 6

978 0 7502 8015 0